Finally, a book launch guide for authors!

M.J. Rose and Randy Susan Meyers offer a guide for authors, covering everything from working with your publisher, to reading in public, to help for publicity and marketing, to using (and misusing) social media, to how to dress for your author photo . . . and far more, including cautionary tales, worksheets, timelines and etiquette tips.

What authors & agents are saying about
What To Do Before Your Book Launch:

"A fantastic resource for every writer in search of an audience. Nuts and bolts, elbow grease, and optimism are on every page of this worthwhile guide. Whatever it costs, it's worth it."

Betsy Lerner,
author of *The Forest for the Trees*

"Every writer trying to sell a story should memorize every word on every page, and never forget them."

Steve Berry,
New York Times Bestseller

"*What To Do Before Your Book Launch* is the new invaluable tool for writers. There is so much to know and now it's all in one place. From now on when people ask me for advice, I'm sending them this book. C'mon! What are you waiting for! You must, must read this!"

Julie Klam, *New York Times* Bestselling
author of *You Had Me at Woof*

"Indispensable take-home value I only wish I had when I was just starting out!"

Andrew Gross, *New York Times* Bestseller

"A few hours after I'd read only a few pages of *What To Do Before Your Book Launch*—on "How to Be Photogenic"—my photo was taken at a group dinner. Remarkably, I had only one chin in the picture, not the usual six! Needless to say, this book is now my bible."

Laura Zigman, National Bestselling
author of *Animal Husbandry*

"M.J. Rose and Randy Susan Meyers are two pros who have been in the publishing trenches, and their guide, *What To Do Before Your Book Launch*, is the best kind of boot camp trainer: purposeful, no-nonsense, and with you along the way, making sure you hit all right moves."

Dan Lazar, literary agent at Writer House

"Essential. Honest. Incredibly valuable and an absolute must-read. This is an open sesame for success—from insiders who truly know the scoop!"

Hank Phillippi Ryan, award-winning
author of *The Other Woman*

"This book is chock-full of great advice for writers—it's now required reading for all of my clients!"

Jenny Bent,
literary agent at Bent Agency

"Dripping with the wisdom authors gain after years of experience but wish they'd had from moment one. If you want to move from book deal to debut in the best of all ways, this book will tell you how to do it—and how not to do it. It is positively packed with essential advice. Highly recommended."

Theresa Walsh,
co-founder of Writer Unboxed, author of
The Last Will of Moira Leahy

"*What To Do Before Your Book Launch* is both brilliant and indispensable. All authors should have it by their bedside. They should read it again, and again, and again."

Joshua Henkin, author of
The World Without You, Matrimony

"Oh how I wish I had *What To Do Before Your Book Launch* before my first novel came out! But I have it now and you bet I plan to use it before my next book publishes. If you're about to launch a book, do yourself a favor: save yourself time, money and potentially years of heartache and confusion and read this book. Then follow Rose's and Meyers' suggestions."

Carleen Brice,
author of *Orange Mint and Honey*
and *Children of the Waters*

"Finally, a comprehensive guide to launching your first book that tells it like it is: What you need to know, do, and be, as an advocate for your own work. *What To Do Before Your Book Launch* speaks the truth your friends are too nice to say and your agent forgets you don't know."

Nichole Bernier, author of
The Unfinished Work of Elizabeth D.

What To Do Before Your Book Launch

VOLUME 1: FOR TRADITIONALLY PUBLISHED BOOKS

M.J. ROSE
&
RANDY SUSAN MEYERS

Cover design by Asha Hossain

Print ISBN 9780985861117

Portions of this book have been previously published in *Poets & Writers Magazine*, *Writer Magazine*, *Writer's Digest Magazine*, Wired.com, the book *The Practical Writer,* and on the blogs Buzz, Balls & Hype, The Huffington Post, Beyond The Margins, and Word Love.

Distributed by Argo Navis Author Services

CONTENTS

Introduction

Introduction

Writers. We get so focused on grinding towards publication that by the time we've finished with query letters, rejections, finding an agent, revising for said agent, Googling the editors on our agent's submission list, waiting for 'the call,' hearing the offer, and then, hallelujah, accepting the publisher's offer, we want to collapse in front of the TV.

Sorry. No can do. During the 2–24 months between signing your contract and receiving your freshly pressed books, there is much to do and little guidance available. For the secrets of debuting, one turns to the underground, where surreptitious bands of debut novelists come together in the shadows to share the secrets they've learned from already published brethren.

Randy's first novel, *The Murderer's Daughters,* debuted in 2010 with St. Martin's Press; her second novel, *The Comfort of Lies,* will launch in early 2013 from Atria. M.J. has sold twelve novels since she first self-published an eBook called *Lip Service* in 1998 (way before it was fashionable). Her most recent novel, *The Book of Lost Fragrances,* is about to launch from Atria as we write this introduction.

The advice and warning that Randy heard from agent Sorche Fairbanks at Grub Street's Muse & the Marketplace

Conference truly informed her future decisions: *No one will care about your book as much as you do. Not your mother, not your agent, and not your editor.* Galvanized by these words, Randy wrenched herself from the dreamlike state in which she creates, and began researching all the ways she could work with her publisher.

M.J.'s mantra is not only her advice; it's the line motto on which she's built her marketing business and the take-away from her career as the creative director at a top NYC ad agency: **no one can buy your book if they've never heard of it.**

So even if you've written the most magnificent book ever created, there's work to be done if you want to find an audience. Done right, you may find a new group of friends, write amazing essays, and learn skills that will serve you well in all aspects of writing.

1

First Steps Towards
Your Book Launch

"We all have a better guide in ourselves, if we
would attend to it, than any other."

— JANE AUSTEN, *MANSFIELD PARK*

What to expect (when you're expecting publication)

First congratulations! This is a very exciting time and you
should savor all the good parts and enjoy them. Celebrate your
getting to this point. Don't over think or over worry what
could go wrong. A lot can go right, and if you are educated
and stay involved, you can help create your own success.

So literally what should you expect? What's going to happen first, and second, and third?

Every publisher's timeline will be different; within your publishing house, every editor will be different, and every client at
that house will probably be a little bit different. With that as a

given, we offer a brief outline of what you can expect from your editor, with the caveat that only your editor, agent, and publishing house can provide you with a timeline you can rely on.

But, in the interest of grounding you before you read on to what *you* should be doing—here is an overview of the most basic steps your publisher will likely take after the contract is signed and you get your first check. (At the end of this book there is a timeline for what you should be doing.)

1. A launch date will be set. It can be a year to eighteen months (or a little more or a little less) ahead depending on the book and the house.
2. Your editor will provide editorial comments to guide you in your first revision. This process could take anywhere from one step to many iterations, as you and your editor go back and forth.
3. Your editor will accept the final manuscript and send it to a copy editor.
4. You'll get another check. ☺
5. About 6–7 months pre-launch your editor will be presenting the book internally at a launch meeting to various departments, such as: Sales, Special Sales, Design, Marketing, Publicity, Audio and Subrights.
6. The cover design will begin. (And later you'll get to approve a final.) This will also happen 6–7 months before publication—usually after that internal launch meeting.
7. You'll receive a copy-edited manuscript (with a deadline). (In time you'll get second pass pages and sometimes third.)
8. About 5–6 months pre-publication you will be assigned a publicist and a marketing person. This is usually 6–7 months pre-launch.

9. Discussions between you and your editor about who to get blurbs from will be initiated. Never be afraid to ask your editor to help here if you don't feel comfortable asking other authors yourself.
10. Galleys (advance reader copies) will be sent out for reviews and blurbs. This is usually 4–6 months pre-publication.
11. At the 4–5 month pre-publication point your editor will present your book at a sales conference to all the sales reps. You should get a copy of the sales catalog including your book.
12. Once sales conference is over, marketing and PR plans will be finalized and your editor will be keeping you up to date about what the house is going to do for your book.
13. About 3–5 months pre-publication, early reviews from the trade will start to come in.
14. About 2–3 months pre–publication, you should be working with marketing and publicity to set up plans.
15. About 6–8 weeks pre-publication your editor will send you the first finished book. (Sleep with it under your pillow the first night you have it for good luck.)
16. Now just wait . . . and make sure you're writing. The best advice both Randy and M.J. ever got was the minute you finish one book–take a few deep breaths and start the next with the goal being that you're deep into the next book when the first comes out so that you won't get paralyzed by all the great praise. ☺

Domain (and other) Names

If you have not yet bought your domain name, immediately, yes, right now—stop reading this—*buy a domain name* for your future website and/or blog. The link provided is a tutorial about the process. Why are you still reading this? Stop. Go buy your own name (if available) in .com, .net, and any other format you can afford. Buy the title of your book(s), and any possible titles you are considering. Buy common misspellings of your name. Buy your maiden name, the name everyone called you in college, every name that you have ever used. This is a business move, not ego. When you create your website, you will be able to make sure all these names lead to your site.

Also make sure to establish accounts in your name on Twitter, Facebook, Google +, Tumblr, Goodreads, Pinterest, and anywhere else you want to have an online presence.

Mailing Lists

Start developing your mailing list the moment you sign your contract. List everyone you know. Find their addresses through the online white pages (you will be amazed how many people you can find). Find their email addresses if you can. People you worked with, went to school with, cousins twelve-times removed, college friends, college enemies, and everyone you ever slept with (come on, they'll be curious, right?). Camp connections. Boy scout troops you led. Congregations. Places you volunteered. People for whom you once babysat. Neighbors. Former neighbors. Everyone. Do a little each day and it will grow. This is the perfect start to your pre-publication work.

Dipping Your Toes in Social Media

Social media is here and it's likely that using it will increase your chances of being read. You don't have to do it. No one will hold a gun to your head. However, at the very least put your toe in the water and try it before eschewing it.

First, learn what you *like* in **social media.** When speaking with other authors we often hear: "I hate Twitter." "Facebook is stupid." "I don't want to blog." "I don't have time for this." Try a different approach. What *can* you enjoy doing in the world of social media? Who do you want to *be* online? Who do you want your potential readers to see? How can you craft that person? (For instance, Randy likes giving advice, researching, and being a know-it-all. *Voila*, her social media persona.)

If you don't offer personality, passion and opinion, you run the risk of boring people. It's obvious when people are posting out of a resentful, "why do I have to do this?" or "let me get this g-d daily tweet over with," or "my damn agent is making me do this." *Hint: If you're boring yourself, you're boring others. (Another hint: Don't denigrate social media to people who do use it. It won't make you look smarter, but it might make users less likely to promote you.)*

Write about things other than yourself. *Meme*, yes. *Me! Me!* no. Everyone expects a new author to promote their book, but if every tweet and FB update is a notification of your next speaking engagement, your latest review, and how dreary the airport is, people will soon roll their eyes when they see your name.

Offer readers something. Readers owe us nothing. Remember, a book is really a product (however artistic the product may be) that you want people to buy. Write your social media offerings as seriously as your other work. Show your voice and your integrity. This is the personality the world sees (and they usually see it before they read your book).

"Work is love made visible. And if you cannot work with love but only with distaste, it is better that you should leave your work and sit at the gate of the temple and take alms of those who work with joy."

KAHLIL GIBRAN

Be positive. Anything you post will live forever. Think about the face you want to present to the world. Complaining and whiny, or upbeat and entertaining? If you want to deprecate, **be self-deprecating.** If you can combine self-deprecating and funny, that's a perfect voice. (Follow author *Julie Klam* on Twitter for a five-star example of this talent.)

Find ways to elicit responses—people enjoy talking about themselves! (For instance, post questions: "What grammatical error irks you the most?" "What's the worst outfit you ever wore while working at home?" "What piece of ancient clothing can you not get rid of?")

There's plenty of social media out there from which to choose. Facebook and Twitter might not be your sort of neighborhood. Investigate other reader and writer sites such as *Goodreads*, *Library Thing*, *Red Room for Authors*, *She Writes*, *Shelfari*, and *Backspace*.

And relax. In the end, this is just a small piece of the publishing pie.

"All that stuff, this public persona of me-let's call him 'the wild man'-that is not helpful. It doesn't make me more of a box office draw. It's the quality of my work that makes people want to go to my films."

RUSSELL CROWE

Social Media Tips

1. Don't be mysterious (*Something wonderful is going to happen to me, but I can't say what!*) It is aggravating, annoying, and implies that you think yourself so important that others will stay awake wondering about you.
2. Use exclamation points judiciously!!!!!!!!!!!!!!!!!!!!!!!! !!!!!!!!! ALSO CAPS LOCK.
3. Don't post anything ugly about other people—this includes personal rants and unflattering party photos.
4. Don't send BLASTS for events or anything else.
5. Don't send group FB messages to your entire following, unless it's a warning that the world is ending and you're the only one who knows.
6. Don't send "thanks for following and/or friending me" with suggestions on how they can follow you even more.
7. Don't put down other writers.
8. Don't write negative reviews of books, or give any book less than 5 stars, unless you're willing to receive the same.
9. Write about books you love.
10. Mention the work and success of others often, with conviction and honesty.
11. Don't change your profile photo too frequently (like weekly) or you may appear self-obsessed.
12. Don't write about your children, pets, or spouse unless you are certain that other people will relate to your story, or find it amusing. (And that your children and spouse will not be offended now or ever. The quickened pulse of a book launch mind can lead to regretful decisions.)
13. Debuting your book is exhilarating, but it's also

exhausting. However, like any performer selling themselves along with their art, unless you can pull self-pity off as funny or endearing, don't let them see you sweat.

Making Friends

Make friends in the writers' community and be generous when you get there. Live by the clichéd but true adage, "Treat others as you'd like them to treat you." Find places online and in real life where you can share experiences, get help, and help others. A few examples of this are: *Backspace for Writers* engenders generosity online writers on all levels of publishing experience. Writers' *conferences* are a great venue for expanding your circle. Writers' communities (like *Grub Street for Writers*) are invaluable.

If there is a conference in your area, be sure to go. This is a perfect place to put out cards, have conversations that may grow into friendships, and find pockets of mutual support. One seminar often generates an ongoing professional network.

Go to readings by other authors, and introduce yourself, making sure to get a card. Then write to the author, letting them know you enjoyed seeing them. Always buy a book! It's rude not to, it's good karma, and the author will notice if you don't.

Reach out. Ask your agent if they know other authors whose books are on a similar publication schedule, or if they have clients with whom they think you will connect. Write to authors whose books you've enjoyed. Post on your blog about books you read and liked. Host a book party for a local author. Frequent a local bookstore so the owner sees you at many readings.

2

Author Websites,
Blogs & Author Photos

Building an Author Website

> "In an abundant society where people have laptops, cellphones, iPods and minds like empty rooms, I still plod along with books."
>
> HARPER LEE

Jealous much? Ah, to have written *To Kill a Mockingbird.* Let's all take a moment to sigh. Most of us would rather be writing or reading, but we're not Harper Lee, so we need a presence out there. (Interestingly, we did find a Harper Lee site, in her name, masquerading as her own site.) So in case you didn't yet, we remind you again: *Go. Buy. Your. Domain Name. Now.*

In readiness for creating your own, begin investigating other writers' websites. Do not wait until the last minute—take your time and do it well. As soon as Randy shook hands on her book contract, she began looking at other authors' sites. You don't have to search for individual authors—most author-website designers include portfolios on their websites.

While you're surfing, note the sites you like. What makes it a good experience for you? Randy likes clean uncluttered sites that are quick to load and easy to navigate. Analyze your preferences. Look at the bottom of the page—note the creators/designers and go to their sites.

If you are the least bit technical, try building a 'beta' site. Randy did this, just using the simple program that came with her Mac. This gave her time to experiment with content and format, and helped alleviate her fear of launching a blog, by allowing her to test it with a small audience of friends and family.

Once you're ready, search the web to find out who is available to create a site, and who you want to work on yours. Establish a budget, but don't cheap out for the sake of a bargain. As your online presence, this is the face you will show the world. Get estimates. Compare what they offer. How about hosting? Site maintenance? Figure out what is important to you. Most authors like having the ability to update their own events, reviews, and news, etc., so look for developers who offer that sort of control.

If your budget is limited, you can go with a less snazzy site—even one you build yourself—and save your money for outreach efforts. You don't have to choose an expensive designer. Websites are like business cards—you need one as a destination, but no one wakes up and says, "I'm going to search out the website of a new and unknown author." So, instead of waiting for them to come to you, go to them with marketing and PR. (More on that later.)

Whether you plan to hire someone to build your site or do

it yourself, you'll need to learn some basic rules for making websites easy to use. There's plenty of good advice available that is specific to this task. Here are two to get you started:

Web Design Hints

Jane Friedman's Author Blog & Website Mistakes

One Truly Key Website Issue

It's not crass to have highly visible "Buy the Book" buttons on your home page with links to your book on Amazon, Barnes & Noble, IndieBound, and a few specific bookstores you love. M.J.'s rule of thumb is that it should take a visitor no more than five seconds to find the "Buy the Book" link on your website.

To Blog or Not to Blog

These days one of the answers to the question, "What should I do to market my book?" is all too often "Go forth and blog." But blogging isn't right for every author.

Overall, nonfiction authors have a much better shot of using blogs to market their books because the books are subject-related and their blogs can easily be focused on a subject. Seth Godin (*sethgodin.typepad.com*) is a great example of a writer whose blog is read for its own sake, and also sells books to his fan base. Godin writes brilliant books about marketing and business, and his blog addresses those topics on a daily basis offering valuable insight and ideas. A blog can go far in marketing your books if you're a nonfiction author with a platform. Think of Arianna Huffington.

Fiction authors can have a harder time finding the right hook for a blog. It can work well for writers who have a strong voice and an entertaining style. Two fine examples are

Jennifer Weiner and *Neil Gaiman*. But keep in mind they've both been writing in this format for more than six years.

Randy's Experience:

My editor and agent offered great advice when I asked whether I should have a blog: "Try it and see if you like it." I first tried blogging on a self-built beta-site, with the challenge of having it live. Knowing I'd be lucky to get even five readers (husband, sister, sister-in-law, older daughter, younger daughter) gave me the freedom to try it.

First, I figured out what I had to say. I didn't want to go by the seat of my pants. I needed structure. I ruled out my life as a topic for a blog. Who cares what I eat for breakfast (oatmeal)? My husband, while he is a source of constant support, doesn't say or do cute things often enough to be the subject of a blog. My kids? They deserve privacy even if I choose to open my own life to scrutiny. Cooking? What do I post once I've recommended Cheerios as the perfect one-bowl supper?

I spent weeks clicking from blog to blog, looking for what drew me back and why, finding that the blogs I visited on a regular basis were ones where I learned about good books and the experience of writing. Thus, I christened my blog "Word Love," figuring that gave me a wide berth.

M.J.'s Experience:

A novelist can use the "platform" approach too. Almost a year before my novel The Reincarnationist was released, I started a blog about the subject of reincarnation which is on the home page of my website. My goal was to make it active in advance of the novel's publication so I'd have a built-in au-

dience interested in the novel's subject. And because this book was the first in a series about reincarnation, I figured the investment would be worth it.

I set it up to automatically feed to my Amazon blog and my Facebook page. I don't use it to sell sell sell—first and foremost, it's an information portal for people interested in past life research. It's a constant marketing tool keeping my name connected to a subject that's at the heart of my recent books.

So we say again: To be interesting to others, write about what interests you. Passion pulls readers in. When we spend time and effort engaging the reader and give the blog the opportunity to grow over time, we can build a relationship with our readers. It's not something you can do in an instant, but if you do a good job and attract a reasonable following, you will have a captive audience every time you publish a new book.

Cross-Posting Your Blog

You can also dip your toe in the water at one of the many sites that allow writers to post on an occasional basis: *Red Room for Authors*, *She Writes*, and *Goodreads* are just a few places where you can put up posts without having to make a large commitment.

If you make the effort to write posts and have a blog, put in a bit more effort and cross-post to sites like those above. Arrange to have your blog auto-feed to your Amazon author page once you have created it (ideally, you will do this the moment your book is available for pre-sale) as well as your Goodreads author page. And consider a multi-author blog. Randy is a member of *Beyond The Margins*; M.J. is a regular at *Writer Unboxed*. Another great example of a group effort is *Jungle Red Writers*.

Try blogging, to see if it appeals to you, but remember: If

it feels ugh, it might read ugh. If that's the case, you should step away. There are many more ways to get your book out there—don't invest time or money in methods for which you have no enthusiasm.

The Blog Trap

Many writers blog about writing. Seems logical, right? It was for the first two or three dozen writers who did it. But these days there are thousands of writers blogging about writing, and while readers might adore our books, it doesn't necessarily follow that they want to know the ins and outs of a writer's life. Not to mention that even our own dedicated fans can lose their taste for our books if our blogs don't measure up—or if we opine about politics when our books aren't political, or religion if we're not writing books about religion, etc. Just because a reader likes your book, it doesn't mean they agree with your point of view. One bestselling author we know shut down her blog after dozens of readers said they'd never buy her novels again, because they were offended by a blog post that had nothing to do with her books.

Blog as Magic Bullet

A few years ago, one of New York's top publishing houses sent emails to hundreds of authors suggesting that each start a blog. They offered free blogging software, with the promise that a blog would act as a promotional vehicle for the authors and their books.

Good idea? Not necessarily.

While it was admirable of the publisher to pursue new ways to market books, we're not sure that putting marketing pressure on an author is ever smart. But more importantly, just writing a blog doesn't mean it will be read. It's the old "if you build it they will come" fallacy. It worked in *Field of Dreams*, but it doesn't apply to blogs.

At last check, *Technorati.com*, a website that covers all things blog-related, tracks more than 112.8 million active blogs, which means there are more people blogging than there are people reading books. Technorati also reports that over 175,000 new blogs are created every day and that bloggers update their pages with more than 1.6 million posts per day, more than 18 updates every second.

Compared to blogs, there are only an average of 500 books published a day. So you could actually have less competition getting attention for your book than your blog. (These figures don't include self-published books. According to industry sources, when those are included, the figure increases to 1,000 books published a day—still far fewer than the number of blogs.)

Time to Blog?

Another blog caveat is that it takes a lot of effort to keep a good blog going. You need to post at least three times every week, and not just a little entry about where you had dinner, how much you paid and whether you'd go back to the restaurant—you need to write interesting and compelling posts that will keep people coming back for more.

On his blog, book reviewer David J. Montgomery said, "Blogging is a colossal waste of time for 90 percent of authors. Any author who launches yet another blog at this point without some unique, exciting and valuable angle is just spinning his wheels."

For a blog to be successful, it has to have passion, voice,

commitment and creativity on a continuing basis. For many of us, that's what writing a book entails and we don't always have enough of those attributes to spare for a blog too.

And according to a 2010 article in *The New York Times*, Matt Richtel wrote that bloggers weren't taking breaks from blogging, which can lead to weight loss or gain, sleep disorders, exhaustion and in some cases, even death.

"A growing work force of home-office laborers and entrepreneurs, armed with computers and smartphones and wired to the hilt, are toiling under great physical and emotional stress created by the around-the-clock Internet economy that demands a constant stream of news and comment," he wrote.

We're all for promotional efforts, but not ones that are detrimental to our health.

Author Photos

Posing for posterity. Is it narcissism or gut-wrenching fear? Except for the most self-confident, most of us begin to think about our author photo about three minutes after getting the publisher's green light. Is this vanity? Only because we pray (sometimes in vain) that our photo will make us seem attractive, warm, and wise; that we look like someone readers would want to have coffee with, or, more important, that double chins won't show and forehead wrinkles will melt under the photographer's lights.

> "To photograph people is to violate them, by seeing them as they never see themselves, by having knowledge of them that they can never have; it turns people into objects that can be symbolically possessed. Just as a camera is a sublimation of the gun, to photograph

someone is a subliminal murder-a soft murder, appropriate to a sad, frightened time."

SUSAN SONTAG

Randy's Experience:

If you're anything like me (neurotic, compulsive), you should start looking for a photographer right away. Ask for recommendations. If you have a relative or friend who has some expertise, consider asking them to help you, at the very least for a trial picture. I learned the hard way. I went to a photographer late in the day, tired, nervous, with the wrong clothes and the wrong attitude. I hadn't thought about what I wanted and I was relying on her to tell me what to do, what to wear, etc.

Five hundred dollars later (and this was a bargain compared to most), I hated all my pictures. I looked like a PTA mom who got some unfortunate Glamour Shots.

Finally, I went to my sister, chastened by my reluctance to take her up on her previous offer (when I was certain that if I paid for the photos, they would be magic). Plus, though my sister is a phenomenal photographer, I worried that with her eye for the unusual and the 'moment' she'd make me look more interesting than pretty, and I didn't care about interesting, I wanted pretty.

Shame on me for not trusting my sister. Jill researched a number of portrait techniques, and between her magic eye and magic lenses, and everything I'd learned from the make-up artists I'd visited, we got a wonderful picture. There's only one problem: I think I look so much better in the photo than I do in person (thanks to Photoshop Botox for Authors) that I am a bit nervous about meeting people in real life.

Research how to look good in pictures. You'll find *plenty* of helpful hints. More than you can *imagine*. For *men* and *women*. Even on *YouTube*. And don't worry about seeming vain. Your photo is going around the world—give it a good send-off.

How to be Photogenic (a compilation of gathered hints)

If you love every picture of yourself, or you're one of those naturally photogenic people, you won't need this. For the rest of us, there are lots of tricks we can use to make photos come out better. After reading the hints below, try on different clothes, jewelry, make-up, hairstyles, and take as many self-portraits as you can stand. Using Apple Photo Booth or a similar program to take photos of yourself in various outfits and poses is the best way to plan your author portrait.

Color counts. Wear the color that looks best on you close to your face. This is the most important thing to do.

Pick the right clothes. Don't overdo it. Avoid busy patterns, large florals, and anything loud. Dress to enhance yourself and make certain your clothes send the message you want to project. What persona do you want to project? Warm and welcoming? Wise? Mysterious? Approachable? Unapproachable? Plan this.

Hide your blemishes. Photos freeze you in time. They can't show all the good (though they can certainly reveal plenty of bad). Learn your good and bad angles and make sure your photographer considers them. Choose a photographer with whom you can be honest. Avoid anyone who intimidates you. Good photographers can work with you to play down certain features and emphasize others.

To hide a double chin, tilt your head down a bit. Not much, or you'll actually exacerbate the problem. Position yourself so that the camera is a bit above your eye level. And there's the old trick of putting one hand under your chin as though you're resting your head on your hand. (Avoid pushing extra skin into weird positions.) Some say resting your tongue against the roof of your mouth helps.

Stick your neck out. Models present a 3/4 pose to the camera, with the neck lifted and the head tilted slightly down. When standing, they place one foot in front of the other and one shoulder closer to the camera. Practice this alone. Trust us.

Relax. Really. Have a glass of wine with your shoot. Just one, though.

Access your inner actor. Imagine yourself somewhere great, gazing at something fantastic. Or, if you're trying to appear mysterious, bring forth the mental scene to engender mysterious feelings.

Choose a smile and practice it. Smile with your eyes. Happiness and warmth are projected through smiling eyes. Imagine someone you love, or someone you would love to love, or someone you want to know, walking in the room. Your eyes will get wider; your smile will become more relaxed. Practice until you can do this on demand.

Sit or stand straight. Don't have your shoulders around your ears or your back slumped.

Make-up for the camera is different than the everyday variety. Visit a make-up counter or Sephora. Tell them you need photo make-up and let them play (it's free, and they'll love the opportunity to demonstrate their skills).

People with lively faces stand a better chance of looking awful in photos, because transient expressions don't come across well when captured in a still photo. Learn how to control your expression in front of the camera.

Look slightly above the camera when the picture is taken to avoid red eye and seem more relaxed.

For full-length photos, position your body 45 degrees from the camera and turn your head towards the lens. Stand with one foot crossed in front of the other and place weight on your back leg. This pose slims and flatters. Pull your shoulders back.

Look on professional photographers' sites for hints on make-up, clothes, and other facets of preparation for a photo session.

Bring a few more outfits than you think you need. Simple, classic looks are best. Oversized clothes wrinkle and make you look heavier in the pictures. Solid colors are best. Wear flattering necklines and long sleeves. Loud patterns and busy fabrics will draw attention away from your face. White or light pastel shirts tend to look washed out. Layers often work well.

Try different looks, such as elegant, edgy and casual. Warm colors or monochromatic tones are often best. For most people, pastels, khakis, oranges and yellows are not flattering in photos. Avoid over-sized, clingy, satin, and shiny clothes. Keep accessories simple.

How Do You Look? (Yes, neatness counts)

Look in the mirror. Do you like what you see? Yes? Great, you're done! But if you could use improvement after years spent writing, living in sweatpants, and letting go of all beauty standards more sophisticated than bathing, consider this: Men, is it time to shave off your beard? Wear a shirt that was manufactured more recently than 1985? Women, do you think mascara is a sin? If not, visit a make-up counter. Shop for flattering and comfortable clothes to wear at your readings. You'll be amazed at how much the salespeople will help you, and the way that these people will become readers and supporters.

Remind yourself that this is not in the service of vanity. (Okay, maybe a little.) You are putting together the image you want to project as a professional author. Plus, how often in life do you get to shop and do your hair and tell the world "it's for work?" You'll be glad you did this preparation when you find yourself facing the camera and/or an audience. Staring. At. You.

3

You're Getting Published—How Lucky Can You Get?

A Cautionary Case Study

No question about it, "Carl" was one lucky writer. At least for a while. At 33, he finished his first novel, *Lucky Boy*, sent out two dozen queries and got an agent within four weeks.

Let's call the agent Lucy. Typically, Lucy gets over 200 queries a week, so this was indeed a lucky break for Carl. Within a month of signing Carl, Lucy had an offer for *Lucky Boy* from one of the better publishing houses for $75,000.

The editor, let's call her Pandora, took Carl to Michael's (where everyone in publishing lunches) and spoke of her vision of the novel, her faith in his talent, and her excitement at launching Carl's career.

Carl was promised that the imprint was devoted to "building a writer's career," not just "buying one book." Pandora told him that the marketing and promotion budget was high and designed to build him a readership.

And then they talked about how hard it is to get published and how many authors would kill for the break that had been handed to Carl on a china platter.

Carl felt as lucky as the boy in the title of his book. But his luck was about to change.

The first sign came when Pandora's assistant called to discuss the edits on his manuscript. "I thought I was going to be working on this book with Pandora," he complained to his agent, after the first few working sessions with the twenty-something junior assistant went badly.

Lucy calmed Carl down, convinced him that the assistant was Pandora's pet and there was no need to worry. "Not a word goes out without Pandora's approval," she promised.

As time went on, it became more and more clear that the assistant didn't understand the book. Most of the changes she wanted didn't make editorial sense to Carl. And then Carl saw his cover, which he felt misrepresented the book.

Lucy told Carl she agreed, but convinced him to accept the cover, saying he was lucky that the publisher was excited about it and it wasn't smart to make a fuss.

Two months later Carl saw his book in the publisher's catalog. It wasn't a full page as Pandora had promised. Nor did it list the ten-city tour or the national advertising campaign that she had promised over that initial lunch.

Lucy didn't return any phone calls or emails for two days, and when she finally did contact Carl, she told him not to panic, that everyone at the house loved the book and he was worrying for nothing. "This is a tough business. You are so lucky. Now's not the time to complain."

It was not the last time he'd hear that in the next eight months. No matter what the problem—the publisher only printing 100 ARCs instead of 500 as promised, the book's launch being postponed to the next quarter, more edits from the junior assistant—no matter how upset he got, the refrain Carl heard over and over was: "But you are so lucky! Your book is being published, that's what you need to remember."

Except he didn't feel so lucky anymore, and when he pleaded with Lucy to call his editor and straighten out the various messes, Lucy finally admitted that she couldn't put her relationship with Pandora in jeopardy.

When the book came out there was little review attention and the initial sell-through was less than stellar. Carl felt anything but lucky. "I became the red-headed stepchild and my book just disappeared."

As authors, are we so lucky to be published that we should shut up and stop complaining? Or should we be angry? Is there a more productive way to navigate this strange land called publishing that does not resemble any other business model?

What's the Problem?

Part of the problem is that it's so damn hard to get published.

"I not only felt a groveling attitude toward my first publisher but also toward my first agent, a woman who sold every one of my novels, but who nevertheless told me at every turn that I was lucky to be published at all, let alone have an agent," said Ada L., a six-time published author.

It took Ada years of prodding from writer friends to ditch this agent and find a new one. Why? She was afraid to call because the agent never had a conversation with Ada without mentioning Ada's "luck" at least once.

Is it any wonder that our primary attitude is gratitude when we are told how lucky we are by countless other writers who are all desperate to be published?

Even seemingly positive news reemphasizes the luck factor. When Oprah picked a book for her book club, other writers talked about how lucky that newly anointed was to be plucked from obscurity.

When the *Today Show* and *Good Morning America* choose a book for their book clubs, every publicist and editor (and again, every writer) talks about how lucky that singled-out author is. After all, with over 130,000 books published a year, you have to be more than a damn good writer to be anointed by reviews, you do have to be lucky to get noticed.

Ada L. suggested that writers don't always feel empowered because we aren't really in on the process. "We don't negotiate, we don't know which editor is looking for which product. We're removed."

One way to empower ourselves is to forget the rules:

"I was told I would never get a review in a major newspaper and not to even try," said Jane T, a mid-list author. "I tried anyway, contacting the paper myself, and when I got the review (a rave) guess what I was told by my publicist? I was *lucky*. And please don't do it again because I was making the publicist's job harder."

ICM literary agent Lisa Bankoff points out that there is also a fear factor that exacerbates the problem. She reports having phone conversations with dissatisfied authors who complain about unresponsive publicists, ill-conceived book jackets, or a lack of advertising.

"Often, they're absolutely right to feel that the publisher

could be doing a better job of it, paying closer attention, offering more meaningful consultation. That said, I've had many of those same phone conversations end with the client BEGGING me not to repeat any of it to the editor. God forbid the squeaky wheel might get replaced instead of oiled."

That fear is part of why we crawl away convincing ourselves we should be grateful instead of acting on our anger. If we get anything—a single ad in a major newspaper, a four-city tour, three weeks of decent co-op in bricks and mortar stores, we consider ourselves blessed. We've heard of too many books that were dropped or just died from lack of publisher effort despite a big advance.

Like abused children we're thankful for every small favor.

In Defense of Publishers

John Glusman, a longtime New York editor, sympathizes with authors and blames a marketplace that is more competitive than ever before. "As a result of consolidation in the industry, there is less of an emphasis on quality and more attention paid to the bottom line. That makes the stakes higher and puts more expectation on certain books to perform."

Publishers aren't out to destroy writers, but publishing a successful book is very much a guessing game. Agents don't mean not to return our calls, they are just overworked. And publicists aren't the devil's spawn who think we are lunatics. They are for the most part overburdened, with too many books to push each month, and review sources that have been truncated from 25% to 50% in the last few years. There isn't time for publicists to do a complete campaign for every book, which is why writers should learn to do their own advertising, or save some of their advance to hire an outside PR firm.

Glusman reminds authors that things that seem personal usually aren't. There are actual problems in publishing today. "There is less and less media attention for books and everyone is becoming anxious. The shelf life and book review space and the attention span of the general public is shorter. And the relatively long time it takes to produce a book makes it even more difficult."

Author Elizabeth Benedict (*Almost, The Joy of Writing Sex*) said that while your book is the center of your world, to an editor it's one of two dozen books she's working on that season, and she knows that not all of those books are going to be smashing successes.

"I imagine that editors keep some distance between themselves and writers so that if a book doesn't take off, the editor can retreat a bit more gracefully, instead of having an author who feels as though the moon has been promised but not delivered. Maybe this feels to some authors as though the publisher wants them to feel 'grateful' instead of involved," she said.

One way to combat this feeling as an author is to have realistic expectations.

Simon Lipskar, a literary agent with Writers House Literary Agency, suggests that when a publisher has paid a modest sum to publish a first novel, it's foolish, no matter how great one's fantasies, to hope that the publisher will print 50,000 copies in hardcover, run an expensive (and often pointless) ad campaign, send the author on an expensive (and often pointless) author tour, etc. "It's the author's part of the bargain as a professional to know that, in most cases, these things will simply not happen. Asking for them, begging for them, demanding them: this is part of what leads publishers to react with an attitude that implies that the author should shut up and take what's being given."

If an author can instead balance expectations against the realities of what the publisher will or won't do for his or her book, then the cycle that leads to feelings of resentment and frustration can be put off from the start.

Lipskar is not suggesting that authors should simply stand back and let publishers do what they're going to do. Rather, he says, one has to be realistic about what the publisher is going to bring to the table and then say, "Okay, so what I am going to do to sell copies of this book?"

Authors who are less frustrated with the process and their publishers are usually of two camps, the bestsellers and those who simply force the issue and get beyond this us vs. them mentality.

Authors who do take control realize that a book is NOT dead after three months (as publishing wisdom dictates), and they get creative. The authors who do not rely on luck tend to have more positive publishing experiences and feel less angry at the outcome.

"What's healthy is to do something about all of this—even if sometimes the only thing you can do is write. I've had to learn that I do have a right to nag my publisher to get back to me in a timely fashion, that I do have a right to nag my agent. It's important to talk. I just had a conversation with my new agent who told me I don't call her enough—I don't complain enough, that it's her job to do these things for me," said Ada L.

What to Do?

Ultimately, we all have to realize this basic truth: If writers don't write, publishers have nothing to publish. And if they don't publish, they don't have a business and we don't have a career. They can't do it without us, and we can't do it without them.

"Without the fruits of your labor, none of us would have jobs," said Bankoff. "I'd have no deals to commission, editors would have time to do nothing but refine their own prose, and the legion of promotion, marketing, publicity and sales people would be forced to invest their energies in other pursuits."

The editor and the agent, Bankoff said, are on a shared quest and it's one only the writer can satisfy. But too often what should be a partnership is not treated as such. It begins with the very way that authors communicate (or don't communicate) with their publishers: an author deals with an agent who deals with an editor. The editor deals with the rest of the house and then reports back to the agent with business matters or the author with editorial concerns. The channels are not very clear.

Glusman suggests that an author rely on his or her agent to make this process go more smoothly. "It's a big universe with a lot of different players in it," he said. "The process itself is fairly simple but there is a lot of competition and every author feels it. An author's agent should be his or her champion, run interference and get involved when there are issues."

Amy Bloom (*Normal: Transsexual CEOs, Crossdressing Cops, and Hermaphrodites With Attitude*) suggests we not be fooled by the nice stuff that precedes signing a contract and that we should proceed through the publishing process with the right attitude. "One can be appreciative without being subservient. Objectively this is a business and publishers are not our parents or our friends, we sell them our goods and they pay for them. We all need to concentrate on doing business in a positive and supportive way. In a way that does not causes pain."

Whoever you talk to, authors, publishers or agents, everyone agrees. It all depends on the agent: you must have an agent you trust.

Being Grateful is a Two-way Street

If all the parties involved demonstrate mutual respect, the idea of being grateful doesn't seem onerous or troublesome. In an ideal world, editors and publishers would be grateful to be publishing, and authors would be grateful to be published, and agents would be grateful to work on behalf of the talented authors they represent.

In fact, many people in the world of publishing are genuinely grateful. Lipskar says he is. "Yes, relationships sometimes get strained, and I certainly know high-handed editors, agents and authors who all think they're bigger than the process. And authors should absolutely be on the lookout for agents and editors who from the outset treat them with disdain. But 'being grateful' can be a positive way of approaching a process that is often fraught with tension as opposed to a sign of codependency and weakness."

Afterword to the above from M.J.

I have never had so few authors and publishing people willing to go on the record or be interviewed as I did while researching this book. Over 50 agents, editors and authors refused. We are in the business of communicating and so this silence is alarming. Such widespread hesitancy to speak about the issue is almost as interesting as the issue itself.

"I don't think I have any right to complain about the things that are wrong—and there is a lot wrong—because I've been so lucky with how my career has gone," said one best-selling writer whose name is known to every reader and every bookseller. "I'd be afraid to jinx it," he added.

Not enough said, but as clear a communication as I've ever read.

More Than Luck: Ten Things You Can Do
For Your Career

1. Bonnie Hill Hearn, author of *The Intern*, who worked
    with writers for over twenty years in her capacity as
    features editor for *The Sacramento Bee*, suggests that as
    authors we should set the tone of the relationship with
    our agents and our publishers at the beginning.

    "It's like a romantic relationship. The problems
    you'll have down the road show themselves in the be-
    ginning; we just ignore them. An agent or editor who
    doesn't return your phone calls or email in the first
    month of the relationship isn't going to improve."

    Poor self-esteem is often the reason we let ourselves
    be treated poorly by those who earn their money from
    us. "I often wonder if we writers spend so many years
    learning to live with rejection, that we accept shoddy
    treatment as our due, just grateful to have any atten-
    tion," said Hearn.

    As in any relationship, remember: you can leave.
    Don't play games. If you say you're going to walk, you
    have to be willing to move on and not look back.

2. Amy Bloom suggests authors ask potential agents about
    the other books he or she is handling and listen hard to
    the responses. Are they selling too hard? Are they talk-
    ing about plans that are too big and unrealistic?

3. Elizabeth Benedict advises authors that they should do
    more than write books. "Write book reviews, short sto-
    ries, essays, travel pieces, anything that gets your name
    out and keeps it there before your book comes out and
    after. It'll make the publisher's job easier, if you've gotten
    some literary attention before." Jonathan Franzen got

attention in this way, with his now infamous *Harper's* essay written before *The Corrections* was even published.

4. It also helps to keep some perspective. "Writing books is a career, not a one-time hit-the-jackpot-or-else pursuit, even though a few people a year do hit the jackpot with their first book. That's rare and it's okay if it doesn't happen to you. What I mean by this is: pick yourself up off the floor and—after you've tended your wounds—keep writing," said Benedict.

5. Gretchen Laskas, whose debut novel was *The Midwife's Tale,* says that you need to do more than just know the people in the editorial and publishing process. "You need to know who these people are as people, and why they are doing what they do. You need to know things that have nothing to do with your individual book (which is hard for writers, or at least it was for me)."

    To this end, Laskas suggests that there is nothing better than (and nothing to substitute for) meeting with your editor and agent in person. "If you are going to be in New York for ANY reason, let them know and ask to take THEM to lunch or coffee. Ask them to talk about why they got into this business, or a book they really enjoyed reading, or what book they are most proud of producing (and do NOT expect them to say your book). In fact, you won't learn as much about them if they say your book."

6. Lisa Bankoff, a literary agent at ICM, suggests that new authors chat with other published writers. "There's nothing like hearing it from someone a step or two or three ahead of you in the process, provided you listen with both ears and can discern the difference between legitimate gripes and sour grapes."

7. Before you choose an agent, Bankoff suggests authors ask about the agent's previous experience in handling his or her type of book. "If you've written a proposal for a nonfiction work of substantive and critical merit, and then given it to someone whose experience is largely in self-help and diet books, they're less likely to know the best editors for your book and less likely to be familiar with how the market will value it."

8. Bankoff also says to pick an agent who suits your temperament. An author who wants to know where and when the manuscript is being submitted and to be kept abreast of responses along the way, should make sure the agent is willing to provide detailed information and communicate frequently.

9. "You want an agent with sufficient experience to bring to bear on helping understand how they (those publishing professionals) approach decisions regarding allocation of marketing dollars," Bankoff advises. An author needs an agent to "make sense out of a business that's still less science than art, a person who will be candid and not cagey about why sales are disappointing."

10. Contact a few of the agent's current clients, advises Bankoff. "Their comments are the litmus test. It's easy to talk the talk, but let's see what happens when it comes time to walk the walk."

Things they don't tell you

(a list from two bestselling writers who wish to remain anonymous).

- They don't tell you that they really only have time to push a few of their titles each season.

- They don't tell you your true print run. (The announced number isn't the same thing as the real number.) And they don't tell you that a lot of your returns get pulped. (Even if they don't have enough books to fill orders.)
- They don't tell you that your book has gone out of stock just as major reviews are appearing, which they could have predicted but didn't take action to prevent. They tell you they have gone back to press and you're elated— woo hoo! Another printing! But they don't tell you that the press run is only a thousand copies.
- They don't tell you that they never sent books to most of the people on your "big mouth" list because they couldn't be bothered or they didn't want to spend the time and money.
- They tell you when a review is coming . . . but then they don't tell you when it's been killed and will never run, even though they know.
- They tell you they plan to run an ad, or include your book in a group ad. . . . but then they don't tell you when their plans change.
- They don't tell you that your publicist is leaving, or has left.
- They don't tell you that your new publicist is still too young to rent a car and has never heard of Somerset Maugham.

NB: M.J. Rose and Randy Susan Meyers are both lucky to have wonderful agents and they have no complaints about their marvelous editors at Atria.

4

Publicity & Marketing

A Quick Overview

No one can buy a book they've never heard of.

So, how do readers hear about books? Everyone likes to say it's word of mouth, but it's not possible to tell a friend about a book until you've heard of it yourself.

That's where PR and marketing come in.

What's the difference between the two?

Marketing is paid placements on blogs, radio, TV, newspapers etc. These show up as ads, advertorials, promotions, blog tours, and more. With marketing, if you pay for it, it shows up. You hire a marketing company and they buy the space. The attention is guaranteed to be there.

Publicity is the opposite. You pay a publicist to pitch your book to newspapers, magazines, blogs, TV, radio interviews and reviews. You are paying for the publicist's effort to get you some attention. A publicist's rate of success is determined by the quality and quantity of her connections.

Should You Hire a Publicist?

You should decide whether or not to hire a publicist early on, especially as the most high-powered ones will want to work with you many (five or six) months before your book comes out. There are different levels of publicists: those who will oversee an entire campaign in concert with your in-house publicist, and those who concentrate on specialized areas, such as radio or blog tours.

Budgetary constraints might be your main concern, but be certain to consider the importance of the marketing side of the business. You have one book getting published and one chance to see it fly (perhaps two if it's coming out first in hardcover and then in paperback).

Many authors decide against hiring a publicist because they're certain "they love me at XYZ Pub House," only to be devastated when they see how thin the love can be in the end. Publicists at most publishing houses are stretched to the limit. The in-house publicist for Randy's first book did a great job, but having an outside publicist from *Goldberg McDuffie* allowed for more in-depth work from both publicists. The two publicists worked together so well that they shared a panel with Randy at Grub Street's *Muse & The Marketplace*.

What About Marketing?

Publicity won't work without marketing.

Just as you can (and sometimes must) pay for an outside publicist, you can (and sometimes must) pay for outside marketing. For most authors, the publisher's marketing budget is limited, so it is important to find out what they are doing and what they aren't doing. Then you can decide how to allocate your money—you might consider anything from marketing professionals to online book tours (*BubbleCow* has a good listing of these sites). You might prepare marketing materials ranging from bookmarks to postcards. Go to online printing sites and you can get lost in the choices. Make sure to prepare at least one good handout and always carry some with you.

> "If you can't describe a book in one or two pithy sentences that would make you or my mother want to read it, then of course you can't sell it."
>
> MICHAEL KORDA

Marketing will provide synergy for your reviews, awards, and good news to make sure that people know your book exists.

Advice from M.J.

While many writers use the words publicity and marketing interchangeably, they're not the same thing and this confusion often causes people to make marketing mistakes. As we said above, marketing is something you pay for. Publicity is something you hope for. They both work to promote a book. People need to hear about a book many times and in several ways before they really notice it.

Marketing is the concrete process of spreading the word about your book by spending money. You can hire a web designer, buy advertising space, and hire a street team. These are all tasks with a specific, measurable outcome. My own marketing business distributes information about books and authors via the web to readers, book club members, librarians and booksellers.

Publicity, by contrast, sounds much sexier. You might get a mention in O *Magazine* or *USA Today*, or get an interview on NPR. Or you might not. Publicists and authors work to generate publicity, but it's never a sure thing. Sometimes these efforts are enormously successful, paying off in high-profile reviews in the *New York Times* and *People Magazine,* but no publicist can guarantee such a reward. So when you put all your efforts into publicity and none into marketing, you're taking a gamble.

How Author Newsletters Can Backfire

By definition a newsletter contains news. To be more accurate, a newsletter should contain news that actually matters to the reader. Of the many author newsletters to which we have subscribed and unsubscribed in the last two years, very few ever held our interest. Only one or two offered any meaningful content.

Newsletters can be very effective marketing tools because they offer direct communication between writer and reader. Your fans have signed up to hear from you. They are hardcore readers. But you have to treat them right.

Newsletters succeed when the author is amazingly entertaining or offers valuable information on a subject in which readers are interested. That subject is rarely the author. Very few authors are so fascinating that people would read weekly or even monthly newsletters about their lives.

Believe it or not, our readers don't usually care to know when we move houses, change our baby's diapers, or receive a prize nomination. There is a fine line between sharing one's work with fans and shoving one's success in their faces. There is a fine line between letting readers know you have a new book out and inundating them with information about that book's shelf life. Your readers want a good read; they want to fall in love with characters or awe-inspiring writing. They don't want 500 words on why you didn't deserve that bad review.

It is very important to recognize that by sending out self-congratulatory or self-indulgent newsletters, we run the risk of annoying and alienating those very precious readers we are attempting to cultivate.

Newsletter Etiquette

1. Do not subscribe people to your newsletter just because they contacted you once. Or answered a note you wrote to them. Don't put your address book into your newsletter database. Let your readers sign up.

   Believe us if we have not signed up for your newsletter, but we once answered your inquiry about our agent's availability to look at your novel, when that newsletter shows up, we know what you've done. And it will probably backfire. If you send an unrequested newsletter, readers might be so annoyed that they avoid your book. Your goal should not be sending a newsletter to 20,000 arbitrary names (99% of who will delete without opening) but rather to have 3,000 dedicated fans who will rush out to buy your new book as soon as you tell them it's available.

2. Do not send out a newsletter just to send out a newsletter. One really interesting newsletter is more beneficial than twelve boring ones. If you focus only on quantity, and send out two or three boring newsletters in a row, your readers will start to think you write boring books.

3. Do send a newsletter when you have a new book out, or are going on tour. Readers want to know that you are running a contest or auctioning off your house to raise money for literacy.

4. Do send out a newsletter if you have a great concept that isn't about you. For instance, if you write dog mysteries, it would be a great idea to do a newsletter on new ways to teach old dogs even older tricks and yes, you can even advertise your own book in the newsletter, as long as it's relevant to the content and you've made the rest of the news (there is that word again) interesting.

As authors, we must remember that although it's possible that our readers will love us (and our work) more if they get to know us better, the opposite is just as likely. Sometimes it's better not to take that risk.

10 Marketing & PR Points from M.J.

1. **No one will buy a book that they do not know exists.** People won't go looking for it if they have never heard of it. That is the goal of marketing and PR: to expose the title, the cover image, and your name to as many people as possible.

2. **85% of all books get less than $2,000 in marketing from the publisher.** And more than 85% of all books sell less than 1,000 copies.

3. **95% of all bestsellers get more than $50,000 in marketing and PR,** and often it's upwards of $150,000. There are never more than two or three books a year that break out on a fluke with no marketing and PR.

When people say, "if advertising and PR worked every book would be a bestseller," they are approaching it from the wrong direction. The real question is, "how many books have succeeded without any PR or marketing?" and the answer is: very few. Advertising and PR can't make every book a best-seller because not every book is good enough or appealing enough. It is much easier to write an exciting ad than to write a whole book. Not even the most brilliant PR and marketing can sell a book people don't want to read. (More on this later.)

4. **PR and marketing cannot make a bestseller, but it is almost impossible to have a bestseller (or a good seller or even a mediocre seller) without PR and marketing.**

Become Educated: There are some great books, newsletters and blogs that can help you. Read and study them. First, you should read my bible of publicity: *Publicize Your Book: An Insider's Guide to Getting Your Book the Attention It Deserves* by Jacqueline Deval. Then sign up for these e-newsletters: *Publishers Lunch* and *Shelf Awareness*. Check out *sethgodin.typepad.com*, *mediabistro.com/galleycat* and my blog, *Buzz, Balls and Hype.*

5. **Marketing and PR are both valuable,** so I advise that if you have a big enough budget you should hire a publicist. For every dollar you spend with a publicist, spend a dollar with a marketing company. That way, even if the publicist can't get reviews and publicity, you'll still get exposure.

6. **Exposure does work.** If you take 100 books and look at the ones that had PR and marketing dollars spent on them and the ones that had none, you will absolutely see that the books that had PR/marketing outsold the others more than ten to one. The problem comes when you look at one book at a time. For instance, I've done *AuthorBuzz.com* and blog ads campaigns where I have proof that over 10,000 people clicked through and looked deeper at the book, but ultimately the

sales were less than stellar. What happened? We got attention for the book, but when potential readers looked more closely, they didn't buy. I've also done campaigns where we did minimal marketing efforts and the book went back to press, which the publisher never expected, or the book listed higher on a bestseller list than they expected or it simply sold through at a better rate than other books in the season/genre.

What happened? It was a terrific book. It resonated with readers. PR and marketing can't sell books. It's worth repeating. PR and marketing can't sell books.

PR and marketing can expose books to potential readers. The book—the words and the premise, the first few pages, the flap copy, the book cover—must entice, enchant, seduce. The book sells the book. In advertising there is a saying—nothing kills a bad product better than great advertising. It's true for books too.

7. **What to spend?** The advice I give everyone, and follow myself, is to keep your day job or a freelance job and spend as much as you can on selling your book. I've worked with authors who spend $985 and others who, between my services and other efforts, spend $50,000. One way to decide is, if you are going to look back and regret spending the money, don't do it. But if you are going to look back and say—if only I had tried maybe the book would have succeeded—then do it. Nora Roberts said you should spend 10% of your advance. For years, James Patterson spent all of his on advertising and kept his job.

8. **Less than a dozen debut books a year break out.** A breakout book is one that sells more than 30,000 hardcovers or trade paperbacks or 150,000 mass markets or about 50,000–75,000 eBooks. Such a book will appear in the *USA Today*, *Wall St. Journal*, or *NYT* bestseller list.

But breaking out is not the only way to success in this business. Your goal as a writer is to keep writing better books and to help those books sell well enough so you can keep getting contracts and writing more books until you write the book that makes a publisher finally say THIS IS IT—then they spend the big bucks and break you out. They say it takes ten years or ten books to really break out. Some people do it faster but some do it slower. Your effort may not pay off on the first book.

Don't worry if you never break out. Many fine writers keep their careers going and are very happy even though their books have never gone above a certain sales level. Not every book has enough mass appeal to soar, but many excellent authors cultivate and maintain a niche audience and have great careers.

It's about knowing your goals and managing your expectations.

9. **If you are going to hire a publicist or marketing firm,** don't believe anyone who promises you specific sales numbers. No one knows how many copies of your book they can move and if they start out by lying, you're going to get screwed. Make sure you look at their testimonials and recognize some of the authors/publishers.

10. **Lastly, if it sounds too good to be true, it's probably not true.** People will try to get you to pay money to attend teleseminars on how to become an Amazon #1 bestseller for ten minutes. All that achievement actually requires is that you manipulate the system and get 100 friends to buy the book within an hour. Don't pay anyone anything for advice like that.

5

How Is Your Book Positioned & How Are You Positioning Yourself?

Case Study: Another Cautionary Tale

Diane L. is an author whose first book sold to one of the best houses in a pre-empt at auction five days after it had been submitted. The excitement was palpable. The foreign rights to the book were sold in seven countries.

When the catalog came out for the book several months later, listed under marketing only one thing was written: publicity campaign. No tour, no advertising, no attention for the title at Book Expo America and no IndieBound support program.

By the time Diane and her agent realized the house had lost interest in the novel it was too late to do any damage control. Partly as a result of the lack of excitement and weak push on the publisher's side, there were no reviews. To date the book has sold 2800 copies.

Her house still published her second book, with no more and no less (could there be any less?) fanfare. It has only sold 1800 copies. They have not made an offer for her next novel.

Diane's sales records have made it hard for her publisher to sell the paperback rights. In addition, her agent is worried about her third novel, which has not yet been picked up. "If it doesn't eventually sell, you'll have to take a significant cut when it comes to an advance," she said.

"I hope my agent can find me a new house and the right editor to stand behind me. But it still isn't easy. I feel like a failure. I feel like I got this big chance to get published and I blew it. It will be a while before confidence returns; probably after my next book comes out and does well . . . if it ever does come out."

What happened?

Diane's first two novels were not published. They were just printed. And that's now the sad fate of too many novels.

Today's Reality

All books are not treated equally despite how well they are written. The majority of novels released today (as many as 75% according to industry professionals) are "printed" as opposed to being "published."

Over 10,000 novels hit the shelves each year—this is up 100% from ten years ago. In that same time period the price of books has gone up as much as 20%, while review space has declined 20–50%. Fewer magazines and television shows will feature authors, choosing instead to feature actors, singers, reality show winners, politicians, or just about anyone else. Book tours, which used to work extremely well, don't have the power or cachet they once did.

Because of these changes and other shifts in the business of books and media, publishers can support only a very small percentage of the books they publish, and more than half of all debut authors never go on to publish a second novel.

In the past, it was assumed that an author who didn't sell a second book just didn't have another book to write. These days it's more likely to happen because the publisher's lack of marketing and support killed the author's career before it ever got started.

Literary agent and author of *Writing the Breakout Novel*, Donald Maass, said, yes. "Authors are washing out faster than ever." Maass attributes some of the change in author circumstances to changes in publishing, but said: "The culprit here is computerized inventory tracking by bookstore chains." Because stores tend to order according to past sales, an author's new book will be stocked according to the sales of her previous title." At the heart of the problem is the fact that there is a disconnect between how the business works and what we as authors expect," said Maass.

Simon Lipskar of the Writers House Literary Agency says that instead of wailing about the state of things, authors should be asking the most basic of questions: "What is this thing called publishing and how can I make it work for me, under my particular set of circumstances?"

What is This Thing Called Publishing?

There is a difference between being published and being printed.

In both cases the book will need a good edit, a good cover, distribution, and a review mailing. But being published also includes a serious public relations effort, a substantial marketing plan, advertising, in-house excitement and involvement, big co-op dollars for the book in-store, and a tour. All of which are costly. A publisher simply cannot afford the $25,000+ it takes to publish each novel it prints. (And $25,000 is the low end—a full campaign can cost $100,000 to $250,000.)

As a result, the majority of novels today are just printed rather than being published.

Being published is the best case scenario, but Lipskar feels that being printed is still far better than any of the alternatives, like self-publishing or waiting to be published until you have a novel that could be bigger or better or more newsworthy.

"If you get a contract and a pub date, count your blessings and work like hell with the publisher to make their efforts succeed. There are things you can do to help your publisher, there are things you can do to complement their work—and you should do those things."

Many authors will attest that their publishers become more helpful once the authors generate some excitement on their own. One author, in preparation for the release of her first book in the fall of 2004, took an online marketing class and created a campaign for her book. This energized her publisher and they increased her print run from 5000 copies to 50,000 copies.

Why You Can Count Your Blessings

"Major publishers have a powerful and unmatched ability to

distribute their products, through their sales forces and relationships with the major accounts. Indeed, they might even be said to have a virtual monopoly on bricks-and-mortar bookstore distribution," said Lipskar.

As a result, even without a big push, a book from a major publisher will be available nationwide in most bookstores.

Another advantage is that publishers create advance reading copies for almost every title in their catalog. "Whether these are ARCs with fancy cover treatments or simple bound galleys, printing and distributing them to booksellers and the media, even without any significant special planning and effort, is expensive and near-impossible without a publisher's resources," Lipskar said.

The review situation is one that can't be overlooked or undervalued. As Lipskar explains: "Being published by a major publisher means that critics and the media in general will take a book seriously. In their minds, it means that someone who's not the author's friend, relative, lover or employee thought the book should be published. Even if you're cynical enough to believe that only authors with those kind of connections to publishers or agents get published, it doesn't matter, because the imprimatur matters to the media. Reviewers treat publishers as gatekeepers in a sense, just as editors treat agents the same way."

Great Expectations: The Writer's Enemy

What should you and your agent do when you find out that your book isn't getting the treatment you'd hoped for? Or even half that? How can you get over the disappointment? How can you save your book? How can you save your sanity?

"I think expectations play a huge part in this equation.

Signing your first book deal is, for almost every author I've met, a major milestone. It feels like the mountain's been climbed—and, from a certain angle, it has," said Lipskar.

Once the author's actually written her book, landed an agent and signed a deal—she's part of a very small select group of writers.

"But," said Lipskar, "publishers have the opposite situation. They've got long lists of books they're publishing. So for them, the pool of books they've got on their list is quite large, and making decisions about which ones to back, which ones to label 'lead' titles, and which ones will receive 'merely' the none-too-paltry minimal publication effort, what we're calling printing, is a tough job."

Even "lead" titles are sometimes demoted. One writer, whose first novel was bought for $250,000, said that he literally watched his editor lose interest in his book as the eighteen months went by. "From when she bought my manuscript to when the book came out, she simply fell in love with another novel. It wasn't anything I did. Or anything I could have done. Her expectations fed mine. And I still haven't gotten over it. It's far worse than a romantic interest losing interest. This was business. This was my editor. Except in the end, she was just as fickle as if this had been a love affair."

In this situation, the author's expectation (and the management or modulation of that expectation) becomes important. Instead of feeling privileged, once the deal is signed, the author should realize that he or she has become one in a large pool of authors with whom the publisher is working.

Lipskar believes that all authors should think that way, whether their first deals make headlines or go unnoticed.

"Instead of thinking, ah, my publisher is going to do it all for me now, the signing of the contract signals the beginning of a new job for the author—she's now a professional author. And there's a lot, I think, that an author committed to her work can do to develop a readership and build a reasonable career," he said.

So, if you sign a deal that does not guarantee major efforts will be made on your behalf, you must limit your expectations of what the publisher will do and what will happen to your next book.

The Care and Feeding of Your Own Career

It's not news, but it's painfully obvious that the ready availability of sales data—whether through Bookscan or a publisher or bookseller's own sales records—has made it far more difficult to keep authors' careers alive when sales decline.

"But, honestly," said Lipskar, "it's just brutal out there; the number of books that are ignored, overlooked, underprinted and undersold are legion, and the only way to combat this is to put aside the wailing and moaning at the publishers—who, for the most part, are peopled by folks who genuinely love books and genuinely want to make money for themselves and for all their authors—and to recognize that the primary responsibility is the author's, ultimately, to look after his or her own career."

In other words: don't wait until it's too late, after the publisher has turned down your option book because the previous book (for which they made only a minimal effort) underperformed and failed to earn out its advance. Anticipate that minimal effort from the start—as respectfully as possible—and do everything you can to make your book work.

Some authors claim that publishers are doing a disservice to authors by making small "printing" deals with authors.

Lipskar doesn't agree. "After all, it's simply a matter of reality that not every book is going to be a bestseller, and it's straightforward business logic for publishers to focus their efforts on the books they are most likely to make lots of money on—though we can argue all day whether their sense of what they're going to make money on is accurate. That said, unkept promises made by the publisher to an author are a huge disservice—that's where this thing can go awry."

When a publisher tells the author they will print 100,000 copies and spend $250,000 on marketing, and ultimately they print 10,000 copies and spend $10,000 or less on marketing, the author may well have been lulled into a false sense of complacency by those early promises.

"One of the things I think a good agent does is filter, analyze and translate the things publishers say to authors so that they make sense and have a context. If, for example, a young but ambitious editor tells his author that his house is behind a book, that there's a lot of attention and buzz in-house, it's important to have an agent who can ask the right questions and find out what that attention and buzz really mean, so that everyone's expectations are grounded in reality, not fantasy."

Editing Your Attitude

Writing is an art. Publishing is a business.

Once you have done your best, bled your heart onto your manuscript pages and struggled to write a book that matters to you, switch hats. Stop dreaming, become a realist. There are several possibilities for your first publication that might lead to a long career. You don't have to get the number 5 slot on the bestseller list and a six-figure advance on your next novel to count yourself a success.

Unfortunately, the mindset of promoting a book is totally

antithetical to the mindset of writing one. And while some authors can do both, for many of us the process of self-promotion is distasteful and disheartening.

Novelist Roxana Robinson (*Sweetwater*, Random House 2003) described the painter John Marin's experience with this contradiction. "When Marin's father suggested that the young artist produce graphic design and illustration work on the side, to support his more creative life as a fine artist, his dealer Alfred Stieglitz responded brusquely, 'That, my dear sir, is like suggesting that your daughter be a virgin in the morning and a prostitute in the afternoon. It's not possible.'"

Robinson points out that publishing fiction today does require this paradoxical approach. "It seems it's our job to figure out how to make it work," she said.

The other problem is our fragile self-esteem and how quickly the mindset of success changes to failure. With each effort the publisher does not make, it gets harder and harder to hold on to our sense of worth as writers.

It's time for authors to own their words in the metaphorical sense. Realize that very little, if any, of the business decisions that befall us are really about our books. Rather they are more about arbitrary forces in the business. It's hard, but it's necessary, for authors to focus on their readers, as the goal of a writer is simply to be read.

A Happier Case Study:

We can all learn from a writer we'll call Alma F.

Alma was thrilled when a major agent picked her book out of the slush pile and called to say he wanted to represent her. Like most of us, she thought she had it made and it was time to start popping the champagne.

Then the agent took the book out to the publishers. Unfortunately, the first three rounds of submission resulted in nothing but rejections: the novel was too small, said one editor. "I loved the characters but not the plot," said another. "I love the plot but not the characters," said a third.

After having submitted the novel to at least two editors at every house, when it seemed no offer would be forthcoming, the agent received a call from a junior editor at one of the major publishers. He wanted to publish the book and made an offer of $20,000.

Alma's agent explained to her that such a small offer meant the novel would not be positioned as a "big" book for the publisher. The book would get minimal publicity, marketing and sales attention. It would, in other words, be printed, not published.

But since Alma and her agent accepted this from the outset, they were able to sit down with the editor and realistically brainstorm about what they could do to push the book.

A plan ensued in which Alma would do some guerrilla marketing and pay for a small book tour (with the editor's blessing).

In the end the book got four nice reviews, and the book earned out. No houses set afire, no bestseller lists climbed, but the novel was a solid success for all involved. Alma was rewarded, thanks to her talent **and** determination, with a more lucrative two-book contract and a solid marketing budget for her next novel.

In today's publishing arena that is a happy ending.

Helpful Hints on Determining Your Path

In general, here are some signals that your book will be

printed and not published and what you need to know no matter what:

1. Enthusiasm. This can't be faked. Listen hard to your editor, agent and publicist. Watch for signs, including early ads in *Publishers Weekly* for your book and the number of advanced reading copies being printed. If the number of ARCs is over 1500, you can be sure that the house is excited.

2. An advance lower than six figures usually means your book will receive minimal publicity efforts, but not always. Ask your agent how many books at your price range have gotten serious marketing from the publisher. That's a better way to judge. Many smart houses are paying less and promoting more.

3. If your editor says that your book will be review-driven, you can assume that the house will not spend money on your book. Discover this early so that you and your agent can make alternate plans (such as hiring some outside help). Understanding what you can expect from the house also helps you to be emotionally prepared.

4. Ask your agent to set up a meeting with your publicist six months pre-pub. If, once you are assigned a publicist, she doesn't return your phone calls, contact your agent.

Author's Note:

Over twenty-five people were interviewed for this chapter, including agents, authors and publishers, but most requested anonymity.

6

Book Trailers, Launch Parties & Public Presentations

Should You Make a Book Trailer?

This is a new area of book promotion that now encompasses awards and a host of online companies ready to provide production. Randy's first book trailer was a surprise from a high school girl who read the ARC of *The Murderer's Daughters*. (It is still on *YouTube*.)

The same talented sister who took Randy's author photo also created a *book trailer*. The sister wrote the copy, together she and Randy bought the images from *Getty* and *iStock*, and a friend composed (and performed) the music. Because Randy was lucky enough to have a talented sister and friend, the cost of the entire production was low.

Should you make a trailer? It seems that YA books now

require this additional piece, but the jury is still out for adult books. Certainly the common "talking head" trailers have never appealed to us—we click them off within seconds. A well-made trailer (funny, enticing, frightening) can evoke the spirit of the book in under a minute and improve your book promotion package. A bad trailer (droning static head) can hurt it. If you have limited money and time, this piece may fall to the bottom of your to-do list. If you are excited about a trailer and have the necessary resources, go for it. But first, watch as many book trailers as you can to figure out what is appealing and what falls flat. Don't let your trailer become a vanity project. It's like a baby—while every gurgle and cheep is fascinating when created by your own offspring, other people's children become boring very quickly. Enlist some outside eyes to help you keep your trailer tight—it should provide a short burst of enticement.

Hint: You shouldn't be the one telling folks how good your book is. Either it speaks for itself, through visuals and copy, or other people's reviews and praise should provide the selling points. This is true for book trailers and also *tweets and other social media.*

Planning a Launch Party

While planning your launch party, you may feel as though you're operating in a vacuum of information. No "bridal magazine" equivalents exist to help plan launch parties. You have to choose a venue and decide how many people to invite, whether to read, what food to serve—it can be overwhelming. And many debut authors haven't even attended a launch party, let alone planned one. It's like being a bride who has never seen a wedding.

If you want your launch party to run smoothly, you must

start planning early. The dreamy stage needs to be gotten through—so give yourself time to fantasize about press coverage and piñatas with books tumbling out, before you get down to reality.

Determine your Goals

What do you want from this party? Lots of book sales? Fun with your friends? Pats on the back? A chance to get drunk and curse your reviewers? A thank-you to all your supporters? Make a list of your personal goals—this will determine what sort of party you plan. Match each goal to an action step.

Right now, as Randy thinks about the launch party for her second book, her goals are:

- Give folks a warm and happy evening.
  (Find a venue with comfortable chairs, great lighting, and a bar.)
- Provide good food as a thank-you.
  (Choose a good local restaurant or caterer.)
- Team up with a local non-profit and match the sales of books for this evening as a donation.
  (Determine what organization would be the best fit for this book.)
- Have plenty of parking and/or be close to public transportation.
  (Be sure to check the location carefully.)
- Sell books.
  (Find a local bookstore—one which reports to Book Scan—willing and happy to bring books to sell. If you sell books purchased with your author discount, they will not count towards your "sales.")

Practical Factors

Money? How much can you spend? This, of course, will be a major deciding factor. Some debut authors think that publishers pay for the party. Perhaps this is true for Very Famous Authors, but most of us just get posters of our covers (and are thrilled with that).

Make a realistic budget, and make that budget work to match your goal. For instance, if your goal is to provide a warm happy space that will leave folks eager to spread the word about your book, making them pay to come through the door will not meet your mission. Cut back in ways that don't go against your goals.

Choose a Venue

You can launch by reading in a bookstore, renting out a top-drawer restaurant, inviting people to your home, or with a number of other events. All bring benefits and deficits; your goals and budget should guide your choice.

Some folks read for the public in a bookstore, and then hold a private party. As with any party, find a space that matches the number of people you expect—not too small so you have to turn people away, but not so large that people feel overwhelmed. If the party after the bookstore reading is close by, you'll need to find a gracious way to handle the transition from store to party.

A major advantage of a restaurant party (and most restaurants are happy to have an event on a Monday or Tuesday night) is that it minimizes the amount of work required. The restaurant provides both venue and catering. But you must be sure to choose a location that provides both a good space for a short program and a comfortable place for mingling. Beware of bars with loud televisions—if your chosen site has TVs, make sure they will be shut off. (And speaking of bars: as long as you provide food, folks are happy to buy their own drinks.)

Make it fun for everyone

Whatever type of event you plan, remember: if you want folks to buy your book themselves and go on to spread the word, make the celebration a joy for others.

If you're agonizing over whether to invite the public, you may be interested to hear about Randy's experience: She sent out personal invites (by email and by post) but also opened it up to the public. Very few people came who weren't directly invited, but for the few that did, it was worth it to her to have put out that public announcement. Book parties don't often draw huge crowds, so unless you're Nora Roberts, you probably don't need to worry about exceeding the room's capacity.

Reading in Public: Ten Hints From Randy

Q: How do you get to Carnegie Hall?
A: Practice, practice, practice.

A reading is often the first exposure many people will have to your work. So, yes, practice will make perfect and the sooner you start the better your performance will be. A few important hints:

1. Don't read longer than 11 minutes; if possible read for less time.
2. Pick a passage that is active. Long literary descriptions do not generally hold people's attention. Practice reading the passage aloud *well* before you debut in public. Get to know the cadence, the places where you often trip up, and the words that require emphasis.

3. Keep in mind that you are performing. Give your audience a great show. You are not doing them a favor; you are inducing them to buy your product.

4. A sense of irony or humor is better than being overawed by oneself.

5. Specificities are always better than glittering generalities. For example, in discussing eating habits, one can say that: *according to a Harris Poll, 3% of Americans ages 8–18 are vegetarians*, or you could say, *many young people today are vegetarians*.

6. If one of your readings draws only a small audience, find a way to make it positive. The first time it happened to me, I choked. I didn't acknowledge it, make a joke, or in any way realize it was my job to ease the tension. (An audience gets tense about the small size of the crowd right along with you.)

   Soon after that debacle, I went to a reading where the author, in a very large room that contained perhaps four people, read from his book, without looking up, for twenty (long) minutes. When he stopped reading, the entire audience (including myself) was enormously relieved—until he picked up another book and said, "I'd like to read something from my other book, XYZ."

   And he read for another fifteen minutes. It was excruciating.

   So, when months later, I found myself facing only two elderly women and one librarian at a reading (which I had driven through snow for 50 minutes to reach), I took charge. First, I acknowledged that, "oh well, it's only us," and then sat down with them. (Being on a podium in front of three people seemed a bit grandiose.) I didn't read. Instead, I gave them the inside scoop on the world of publishing. We had a wonderful time, they bought my book, and everyone went home unembarrassed.

7. Prepare written talking points for your non-reading presentation to avoid droning and repetition (often symptom of ill-preparedness). Know what you are going to say and in what order you expect to present it. I have a variety of 'talks' written out, which I've practiced enough that I can give the presentation by glancing down and seeing what comes next. Extemporaneous comments can be good, but a well-thought out, interesting talk is always better.

8. Research. Listen to other authors speak. Being part of an audience is the best way to learn what works and what doesn't in a public reading. Does it feel as though they're reading too fast? Too slowly? Are you drifting off? Why? Analyze your reactions, and then see how you can apply that knowledge to yourself (and *always* buy their book if you want to protect your karma).

   Practice reading in front of friends and family. I asked a group to be my 'beta' audience, trying out various sections to see which was best to read aloud. Many of my favorite sections didn't work, such as passages of description, and parts that, out loud, were undecipherable, especially lacking the knowledge of earlier passages. Parts which might have been alliterative or poetic didn't capture an audience's immediate interest when read aloud. Please your audience, not yourself.

9. Buy *Naked at the Podium*. This tiny book will prepare you for all aspects of your public appearances.

10. Wear lovely and professional clothes. And comfortable shoes.

7

Ms. Meyers—
Manners For Authors

As I waited for my book to launch, I was told by the experienced, "*Don't expect to get on Oprah.*" (I wasn't.) Many said that waiting was "*the quiet before the quiet,*" (hey, thanks for depressing me!) that, "*You don't need to spend money on an outside publicist*" (*very* glad I ignored that one) and, my personal favorites, "*Don't get too excited*" and "*Don't pay attention to reviews or Amazon numbers.*" (To which I should have answered: *where should I get the lobotomy?*)

Which taught me this: Sometimes people are speaking from sour grapes, sometimes jealousy, and sometimes you're simply dealing with an Eeyore. Sometimes folks are helpful; sometimes they're not. Some will spend their time telling you, in gushing terms, how much their 'they-love-me-to-death' publisher is doing for *them, them, them*! You'll soon learn to identify these types.

When my grandmother turned 97 we had a party for her. (Why at 97? We are an odd, odd family.)

"*Grandma,*" I asked, "*what's your very best advice for life?*"

She looked at me, this warm woman who'd never complained about a person in her life (I am actually not certain she is my biological grandmother, whereas there is no doubt that I received genetic material from my card-sharking kleptomaniac Grandma) and she said, "*Be nice to people.*"

I am certain there are a number of snappish authors who advocate that dogs-should-eat-dogs, who have managed to hit every bestseller list, but I believe in nice. I recommend that 'nice' (which, by the way, is entirely unlike being a doormat) color your launch.

Get into training now. Answer your mail. All of it. When you receive a compliment, say thank you. When a reader complains that you are biased, don't rant at your accuser (especially in public!). Ignore them or try to answer thoughtfully. I sent one such email to an angry woman who'd written to me because she thought I'd been disrespectful at one point in my book, and received a more rational answer. We actually found some common ground.

I've read postings by debut authors grumbling about the letters they receive. *God, I can't believe what these people write to me. They want a book! They want a signature! They want me to speak to their class!* Perhaps this public complaining is a way of showing off how *Very Important* one has become. Or perhaps they really are stretched to the limit. Too bad. Every job has its down side, but do you want your doctor to write about how disgusting she found your rash?

Don't grumble in public. Especially in print. Never online. And never about your fellow writers. (Unless you are looking to build a reputation contingent on your cruel wit. Some do. This is not recommended for the average sarcastic person—be certain you are nasty and anti-social enough to pull this off this snarky persona.)

I don't give bad reviews. If I don't like something, I keep it to myself—I never post a negative review on Amazon or Goodreads, or anywhere else. Not because I'm too wimpy to be honest, but because there are enough professional and amateur critics out there and I know how much even the best-intentioned criticism can hurt, and I don't want to add one more bad word. I either give five-stars or I don't do anything. And trust me—writers notice. When I get a 4-star review on Amazon from someone I know, oh, I notice. Never underestimate the thin skin or pettiness of your fellow writers.

Do you plan to write about your life as an author? Readers—and you are seeking readers, folks, not just the guffaws of your fellow writers—don't want to hear complaints about how tired you are, how much you hate writing, and what a grind revision is. It's better not to show how the sausage is made.

The proper audience for swearing about critics, cursing about Amazon reviews, or sneering at the efforts of more successful writers is your trusted team of writer-friends. And if you have complaints about your treatment at the hands of your publisher, take them to your agent.

Don't, don't, don't whine in public! You have published a book. This is a fantastic feat. Let people see how happy and grateful you are. I may have broken this rule during the Macmillan-Amazon contretemps, which occurred very shortly after my launch. The corporate wrangle resulted in the inactivation of the 'buy' button' on my book's Amazon page. I wrote a *post* about it, but limited my comments to my own experience, seeking to be interesting, not to vent anger or assign blame. Did I succeed? Maybe, maybe not—but the article was cited by *Guardian UK* and *The Christian Science Monitor*, so I'm awfully glad I didn't embarrass Grandma.

Don't forget to thank your agent, editor, copy-editor, cover designer—everyone. Flowers, candy and bagels are all nice. Paperweights. Wine. Etsy is a perfect source for unique gifts.

Last piece of how-to-be-nice advice: Readers don't limit themselves to just one book. (Not even yours.) If you are a writer, you are probably also an avid reader. Publicly praise great books you read. Use Facebook and Twitter to spread good words about other writers. Promote their books—even ones that come out the exact same week as yours. It's good karma. You can't expect help if you don't provide it to others. And it's nice. Just like Grandma said.

8

Consolation For
Bad Reviews

The awe you feel at seeing your book on a shelf will be balanced by despair when you read the word "blech" in a reader's review. It's a necessary part of the business, but it hurts. Writers (from *NYT* bestsellers to brand-new authors) must find ways to soothe the inevitable pain of a bad (or even indifferent) review.

We come bearing the intellectual equivalent of brownies (or tequila shots, depending on your chosen vice)—sometimes only the comfort of "misery loves company" can help. We'd offer mead to Shakespeare, had he lived in the time of Amazon and read this review of *Romeo and Juliet*:

"As far as I'm concerned, the only good thing about "Romeo and Juliet" is that it spawned the plot for "West Side Story," which, although laden with cheese, does highlight some of the more noble facets of the human character (along

the less noble) and features some wonderful music. "Romeo and Juliet" will, however, simply annoy anyone with half a brain."

That first angry reader review usually shocks the author. They may be less literary than critical professional reviews, but anonymous Internet reviewers will go where NYT reviewers would never tread.

One newly published author privately spilled her horror to a group of fellow writers when she found this on a popular book site: *"To those who loved this book, may we never meet on subway, train, or plane."*

The unsurprised writer friends, as always, gathered around the new author and shared their own hurtful reader reviews, which we will share with you for your own moment of need:

"Someone once hated one of my books so much that she made a custom e-stamp that said, "This book is so bad it should be banned from the face of the earth."

"There is just no level on which this book was not bad. Bad, bad writing."

One writer's book was placed on a reviewers *"crap-i-couldn't-finish shelf."*

Another was told, *"This author had no right to write this book because she doesn't really know what it's like to be divorced. I went to school with her and I know for a fact she's never been divorced."*

One book was compared to a Tampon ad.

If you ever find yourself on the verge of a decline after receiving an awful online review, look up a classic, a best seller, a book you love, and read Amazon reviews such as those below (sic included). Remind yourself that you may be miserable, but you are in truly excellent company.

Reader Review of Wuthering Heights

I began reading–"though you mayn't believe it," to quote Lewis Carroll's Mock Turtle–at the age of 1 and 9 months. Since then I have read literally thousands of books. And of them all, "Wuthering Heights" is my least favorite. The characters are so unpleasant and cruel to each other that reading the book is a seemingly endless nightmare.

Reader Review of 1984 by George Orwell

Only read this if you like getting depressed. This is a good example of the fact that pessimistic and shocking books often receive rave criticism while dynamically optimistic books are dubbed "unrealistic" . . . NO further comment.

Reader Review of Anne of Green Gables

Here is what most people and fans don't know about the author:

Lucy Maud Montgomery was into the occult and worshipped nature. She taught girls how to make a "table rap" or to call up an evil spirit, and she introduced the Ouija board to the young fry of Cavendish. I believe that her books are "blessed" by an evil force, which is part of the reason that they (her books) have millions of fans. Lucy Maud's ungodly beliefs appear often in her writings.

God opened my eyes to the bad influence of Anne Shirley and her author, and also to all the wrongs in L.M. Montgomery's books.

Reader Review of Goodnight Moon

We were given this book as a gift. I really dislike it–there seems to be an unpleasant undertone: "bowl full of mush," "goodnight nobody." I find the illustrations equally unpleasant (or maybe that's why I find the book unpleasant). I recycled it.

Reader Review of Tale of Two Cities

I feel this could have been a better book had he not been paid for its length. It takes him too long to say simple things. If you hated Old Man and the Sea, you too will hate this.

9

Randy's Ten (Book Launch) Commandments

As I counted down the days to publication of my debut novel, my every moment was filled with panic. How would I cope with bad reviews? (Weeping. Definitely weeping.) What if I got NO reviews? (More weeping.) What if no one came to my book launch party? What if there was a blizzard that night? What if the food ran out? (Tears, fits, sobbing.)

Another worry that recurred in those days: What if I behaved badly? I've learned almost everything I know from books, and though there are many on my shelf with advice on writing, selling, promotion, grammar, and even the giving and taking of criticism, I've yet to find a guide to the proper etiquette of launching a book (and this seemed especially necessary at that time, when self-absorbed monsters screamed *me, me, me,* in my head).

There was no rulebook, and though I was raised without formal religion (except bagels and lox) I know that many look to their God for wisdom. Thus, when I was in need of rules, what better template to use than the Ten Commandments? These are my Writer's Launch Commandments, humbly based on the policies received by Moses and adapted to address all I've witnessed (the good, bad, and clumsy) in others and myself:

1. You shall have no other gods before . . .

Remember your agent: She who brought you into this world, she who rescued you from the mud, dragging you by the strength of her strong and motherly arms, and introduced you to your editor and publishing house. Consider her wisdom first and always in your decisions.

2. Beware blasphemous words . . .

Swallow your rage when your book is spurned by the mighty *New York Times Book Review*. Remember the flood of clients above which your publicist must swim. Do not imagine yourself more worthy than your neighbor. Your publicist must spread her love wide.

You must remember, you are as a child in this business: suck it up and stand in line.

3. You shall not take the name of the Lord in vain . . .

Never speak ill of your publisher or editor, for it shows naught but crass ingratitude and will come back to you threefold. If you propagate evil on the Internet, you are too stupid to deserve a second chance.

4. And on the seventh day, rest . . .

If you do not turn your head away from the screen, and refrain from checking your Amazon statistics, your arm will be as stone and your advance will be wasted on massage therapy and ibuprofen.

5. Honor your father and your mother . . .

Drink not of your own Kool-Aid. Your husbands, wives, children, and siblings exist beyond your sphere. Treat *not* your family as your entourage. Do not expect them to read every word you write, unless you plan to admire every database they build, every car they fix, and every throat culture for which they swab.

6. You shall not murder . . .

You shall not kill your friendships through neglect or blasphemy, by speaking of your book launch as an event to equal their baby's birth, or by forgetting their upcoming nuptials because you were busy trying make-up techniques for your next author photo.

7. You shall not commit adultery . . .

You must not betray your own loyal companions, in fact or imagination, when tempted by the agent, editor, publicist, or marketer of another, no matter how mightily they work on behalf of their authors.

8. You shall not steal . . .

Do not take the words of others for your own. Upon reading a brilliant tweet, you may only retweet.

*9. You shall not bear false witness against
your neighbor . . .*

Speak well of your fellow writers. They are your sisters and
brothers. Bringing another down will not raise you up.

10. You shall not covet your neighbor's . . .

You may not compare the sales rankings of your sisters and
brothers with your own, for it will bring you only madness.

10

A Timeline for the Year Before Publication

Below is a compilation of the previous chapters, which can be used as a checklist.

This list supposes that the author has an in-house and/or outside publicist and marketing person. Below are the responsibilities of the author.

One year (or sooner) before publication

- Buy domain names:
  - Your name
  - All variations and obvious misspellings of your name
  - The title of your book
- Ask your editor for a preliminary calendar of dates (s/he can provide a launch date schedule, submission and edit-

ing deadlines, jacket planning, when catalogs are made, sales reps schedules, galley dates, shipping dates.) You probably won't get hard dates at this point, but even a general outline will be helpful.

- Prepare a publicity kit, including:
  - Book synopsis & bio (long, medium & short version).
  - Create a 'news and praise' sheet with blurbs & reviews, and update periodically.
  - Covers: Foreign & domestic.
  - Book announcements and letters to include with ARCs and review copies of your book.
- Begin to compile mailing lists (email and postal).
- Visit author websites for ideas.

Eight months before publication

- Have your author photo taken.
- Work with editor and list people you know for blurbing your book.
- Investigate outside publicists & marketing firms.
- Identify web designers.
- Prepare "Reader's Guide."

Six months before

- Ask to see catalog copy for your book.
- Meet with inside publicist & marketing person from publisher.
- Hire outside publicist and marketing company.
- Hire web designer to create your site or begin designing your own site.

- List people who should get advanced reading copies (ARCs).
- Make announcement (FB, email, Twitter, etc.) when your book becomes available for "pre-sale."
- Check the accuracy of your book information at online sites.
- Give publicist list of bookstores and other venues for readings.
- Choose online book tour sites.
- Draft material for jacket copy. The editor will write the final version, but her job is easier with your material in front of her.

Five months before

- ARCs begin to go out—decide how to use your author copies. Publicist & editor will send out for reviews and blurbs.
- Check ARCs recipient list, add your names to publicist's and emphasize important sources.
- Begin planning launch party.
- Check all press materials prepared by publicist, editor, marketing team, etc.

Four months before

- Finalize book tour plans.
- Book venue, caterer, bookseller for launch party.
- Prepare website to go live.
- Work with publicity and marketing on final plans.

Three months before

- Make website available online.
- Reach out to other writers and blogger for guest spots to coincide with your launch.
- Identify niche publications and sites where your book will be of particular interest (anything that fits the theme of your book).
- Write letters to old friends, alumni groups, anyone you want to notify personally.
- Work with PR person to identify ways you can fit into news, lifestyle, op-ed, or feature stories.
- Review press releases created by PR person.
- Create party invitations.

Ten weeks before

- Prepare final schedule of events, readings, parties, etc.

Two months before

- Finished books should be ready. Send copies with a personal note to those who've helped you, all who blurbed you, and anyone you think will pass the word.

One month before

- Write op-eds, columns and essays connecting your book to current events.
- Ensure tour schedule (on line and physical) is in order.
- Have outfits for readings and events bought and ready.
- Send out invitations to book party.

Countdown to Launch

- Send email announcement of book launch.
- Post social media announcements of book.
- Ask *close* friends & relatives to announce book launch.
- Smile.

11

Worksheets for Social Media

Social Media Voice Worksheet

Determining Your Mission, Goals & Strengths, and Strategies

1) Mission—State your general purpose, such as: "I want to sell books" or "I want to build a presence/name so agents will notice me"

   I will/do participate in (FB, Twitter, etc.) in order to_____

2) Goals—Create some specific milestones you hope to reach to fulfill your mission, such as: "I want 1000 regular readers on my blog"

   Steps I will take to implement my goals are

   _____

3) Strengths—Identify what you are good at, and what is

interesting about you, that will help you meet your mission and goals, such as:

My most significant areas of expertise are

_____

4) Strategies—Choose the methods you will employ to reach your goals, such as: "Identify the most interesting aspects of my personality which I can highlight online"

The strategies I can best employ are

_____

Determining Your Online Voice

What Can You Offer?

If you want them to come, once you have built it, you have to know what you can offer. Below is a simple set of questions to help you determine what you can offer with passion, expertise, and enjoyment. Your abilities and happiness should direct your online presence.

1) My favorite activity is:

2) I am most passionate about:

3) I am skilled at:

4) I do NOT want to share:

5) I love sharing:

6) Friends and family often ask me about:

12

Writers on the Craft & Business of Writing

On Revision:

"Cut it by 10 percent. Cut everything by 10 percent . . . Cut phoniness. There are going to be certain passages that you put in simply in the hope of impressing people. It is true of me, and it almost surely true of you. I have maybe never known a writer of whom it is not true. But literary pretension is the curse of the postmodern age. We all have our favorite ways of showing off and they rarely serve us well. When you have identified your own grandiosity, do not be kind."

The Modern Library Writer's Workshop: A Guide to the Craft of Fiction, by Stephen Koch

"The only way to improve our ability to see structure is to look harder at it, in our own work and in others'. When you read a book you love, force your mind to see its contours. Concentrate on structure without flinching until it reveals itself.

Text is a plastic art, not just a verbal one: it has a shape. To train your mind to see shapes more easily, write them (and sketch them if you like) in a notebook. As with writing down dreams, the more you write, the more you will see."

The Artful Edit: On the Practice
of Editing Yourself, by Susan Bell

On Craft:

"Significant detail, the active voice, and prose rhythm are techniques for achieving the sensuous in fiction, means of helping the reader "sink into the dream" of the story, in John Gardner's phrase. Yet no technique is of much use if the reader's eye is wrenched back to the surface by misspellings or grammatical errors, for once the reader has been startled out of the story's "vivid and continuous dream," the reader may not return."

Writing Fiction, by Janet Burroway

"What is the throughline? Throughline is a term borrowed from films. It means the main plotline of your story, the one that answers the question, 'what happened to the protagonist?' Many, many things may happen to her—as well as to everybody else in the book—but the primary events of the most significant action is the throughline. It's what keeps your reader reading."

Beginnings, Middles and Ends, by Nancy Kress

"Imagine you're at a play. It's the middle of the first act: you're really getting involved in the drama they're acting out. Suddenly the playwright runs out on the stage and yells, 'Do you see what's happening here? Do you see how her coldness is behind his infidelity? Have you noticed the way his womanizing has undermined her confidence? Do you get it?' . . . This is exactly what happens when you explain your dialogue to your readers."

Self-Editing for Fiction Writers,
by Renni Browne & Dave King

" . . . the quickest and easiest way to reject a manuscript is to look for the overuse, or misuse, of adjectives and adverbs."

The First Five Pages: A Writer's Guide to Staying Out of the Rejection Pile, by Noah Lukeman

"Because fiction requires a mighty engine to thrust it ahead—and take the reader along for the ride—backstory if used incorrectly, can stall a story. A novel with too little backstory can be thin and is likely to be confusing. By the same token, a novel with too much backstory can lack suspense. . . . Remember this: The fantasy world of your story will loom larger in your imagination than it will on the page. . . .

"Balance is the notion that every element in the story exists in its proper proportion . . . When you lavish a person, place, or object with descriptive details, readers expect them to have a corresponding importance."

Between the Lines: master the subtle elements of fiction writing, by Jessica Page Morrell

On Tension:

"Inner censors interfere with effective revision in a number of ways. For instance, most fiction writers act like protective parents towards their characters, especially the hero and his or her friends. Writers are too nice. You not only don't have to treat your characters nicely, in revision you should look for ways to make the obstacles bigger, the complications seemingly endless, and their suffering worse. Avoid the temptation to rescue your characters."

Manuscript Makeover: Revision Techniques
No Fiction Writer Can Afford to Ignore,
by Elizabeth Lyon

On Sex:

"Sex is not an ATM withdrawal. Narrate from inside your characters' bodies and minds, not from a camera set up to record the transaction."

The Joy of Writing Sex, by Elizabeth Benedict

On Public Reading:

"Few writers are truly gifted at giving readings, and most have panic attacks before doing an interview, whether for radio, print, or television. And nowadays an author who isn't deemed 'promotable' can be a liability . . . It's important to plan your readings and selections before you speak in public. Long descriptive passages usually put people to sleep, as does staring down at your book for twenty minutes and reading either too fast or in a monotone . . . provide some meaningful stories. If an audience has come out to see you, give them something they won't find in the book."

The Forest for the Trees, by Betsy Lerner

"Presenting the character of 'you' can be tricky indeed. Unless you are a natural ham or have a kind of droll persona you use at parties, the best way to develop your 'character' for readings is to focus on the material you're presenting and let the subject matter become the character."

Naked at the Podium, by Kahle and Workhoven

On Environment:

"In truth, I've found that any day's routine interruptions and distractions don't much hurt a work in progress and may actually help it in some ways. It is, after all, the dab of grit that seeps into an oyster's shell that makes the pearl, not pearl-making seminars with other oysters."

On Writing, by Stephen King

On Promotion & Marketing:

"Increase your exposure by traveling with another author, even if you have different publishers."

Publicize Your Book by Jacqueline Deval

"I'll let you in on every publicist's dirty little secret: media alone cannot a bestseller make. We publicists take a certain martyristic pleasure in thinking that every book lives and dies in our lap. And while I wouldn't sneeze at the chance for a *New York Times* book review, or a stint on NPR, or a morning show booking, the truth is that none of them—or even all of them together—will necessarily skyrocket a book to success. Publicity is merely a means to an end . . . and that end is something called "buzz.""

The Savvy Author's Guide to
Book Publicity, by Lissa Warren

On Sustaining:

"You have to remind yourself that it's very hard work. If you drift along thinking you've got some sort of gift, you get yourself into some real trouble."

Arthur Golden

"I try to remember that a review is one person's opinion—and a cranky person's at that."

Elinor Lipman

"I would go anywhere, to anybody who wanted to give me a book party. I started taking my books to beauty shops. I did a lot of Black Expos (African American trade shows). I'd be there two days, and I'd be lucky to sell fifty books."

From *The Resilient Writer,*
edited by Catherine Wald

"Over the years, I have calculated that feedback on any given piece of writing always falls into one of three categories, and breaks down into the following percentages: 14 percent of feedback is dead-on; 18 percent is from another planet; and 68 percent falls somewhere in-between."

Toxic Feedback, by Joni B. Cole

"I know there are authors who find it healthier for them, in their creative process, to just not look at any reviews, or bad reviews, or they have them filtered, because sometimes they are toxic for them. I don't agree with that kind of isolation. I'm very much interested in how African-American literature is perceived in this country, and written about, and viewed. It's been a long, hard struggle, and there's a lot of work yet to be done. I'm especially interested in how women's fiction is reviewed and understood. And the best way to do that is to read my own reviews."

Toni Morrison, *Salon Interview*

About the Authors

M.J. Rose is the internationally bestselling author of 12 novels (most recently *The Book of Lost Fragrances*, published in March 2012) and two nonfiction books including *Buzz Your Book*, co-authored with Douglas Clegg. Her novel *The Reincarnationist* was the basis for the Fox TV show PAST LIVES. Rose was a founding board member of ITW. She has appeared on The Today Show, CNN, Fox News, and All Things Considered, and published in the *NYT*, O magazine, *The Wall St. Journal* and more. Rose was the creative director of a top NYC ad agency and created Authorbuzz.com, the first marketing company for authors. Follow her on Twitter *@M.J.Rose*.

The drama of *Randy Susan Meyers'* novels is informed by her years spent bartending, her work with violent offenders, and her years spent loving bad boys. Raised in Brooklyn, Randy now lives in Boston with her husband and is the mother of two grown daughters. She teaches writing seminars at Boston's Grub Street Writers' Center. Her debut novel, *The Murderer's Daughters,* an international bestseller, was chosen as a "Target Club Pick," and a best book choice by *Elle* France, *Daily Candy, Goodreads, The Boston Herald, The Winnipeg Free Press,* and *Book Reporter*, among others. Her new novel, to be published by Atria in early 2013, is a story of three women whose lives became intertwined due to their shared connection with a five-year-old girl: Tia, pregnant by her married lover, gave the baby up at birth. Juliette was unaware her husband had fathered this child, until now. And Caroline, pressured to adopt the child, never felt she could be a good mother. *The Comfort of Lies* is the story of the year they meet.

Made in the USA
Lexington, KY
02 October 2012